SHOW AND TELL

HOW TO SHOW AND WHEN TO TELL

WRITING LESSONS FROM THE FRONT
BOOK 16

ANGELA E. HUNT

HUNT HAVEN PRESS

The **Writing Lessons from the Front Series**

A Christian Writer's Possibly Useful Ruminations on a Life in Pages,
supplemental volume

The first ten books are available in one volume, **Writing Lessons from the
Front,** the first ten books.
Paperback ISBN: 978-0692311134
Hardcover ISBN: 978-1961394100

Visit Angela Hunt's website at www.angelahuntbooks.com.
Show and Tell, Copyright 2025, Angela Hunt.
Published by Hunt Haven Press. All rights reserved. Do not reproduce or
share these pages without permission from the publisher.

ISBN: 978-1961394896 paper
978-1961394919 ebook

SHOW AND TELL

HOW TO SHOW AND WHEN TO TELL

WRITING LESSONS FROM THE FRONT
BOOK 16

ANGELA E. HUNT

INTRODUCTION

Show, don't tell.

E. L. Doctorow said, "Good writing is supposed to evoke in the reader—not the fact that it is raining, but the feeling of being rained upon."

Short of splashing your reader with a cold cup of water, how are you supposed to do that?

Like all the books in the **Writing Lessons from the Front** series, this lesson aims to teach the foundational principles, so you can confidently write your story.

Let's jump in.

THE FOUNDATIONAL PRINCIPLE

Repeatedly, we writers are urged to "show, don't tell." But this ubiquitous advice ignores the fact that there *is* an appropriate time for telling. If we *showed* every single cause and reaction in a story, if we *showed* every element in a room or every expression that crosses a character's face, our books would be thousands of pages long and nearly impossible to read.

So let's stick to the foundational principle: **when the information you wish to impart is intellectual, distant, or simply factual, tell it.**

If that information should evoke an emotional response in the character or the reader, show it.

Simple.

But pondering this question can drive you a little crazy when you're neck deep in a first person book where your protagonist is relating her story and your critique group complains that the entire book is "telling."

Is it?

Any first person protagonist will share his or her story with the reader, but *telling* is the wrong word. In first person, a character *narrates* his story, and the writer, standing in for the protagonist, should follow the same principle mentioned above: if the information is primarily factual, it can and should be told. If the information is primarily emotional, it should be shown with enough sensory details to make the reader feel as if she is in the scene.

Telling, showing, and narrating. Let's learn how to do these three things well.

WHEN TO SHOW

You should employ *showing* techniques whenever you want to immerse a reader in a scene—when you want your reader to hear, smell, taste, touch, and feel the sensory details of your character's environment. Showing will slow the pace of your story and heighten the reader's feeling of participation. When you use showing effectively, you'll get reader reviews that say, "I felt like I was there!"

That's a good thing.

But showing is not always appropriate. Sometimes you don't want to slow the pace of your story, and at other times you may want your reader to feel detached from the scene, or not present in the story action at all. At times you may want your protagonist and the reader to know something that happened in a battle two hundred miles away, but your reader doesn't want to experience a scene that has only a passing connection to your story.

More on that later, because this section is about *showing*.

Most beginning writers set out to tell a story, so they do. Suppose you write this as a first paragraph:

John Smith was an ordinary man who lived in an
ordinary house on an ordinary street. He had a
brunette wife he adored, and two red-haired children whose origin he occasionally questioned.

Interesting enough, but rather bland because you are
telling me about John Smith. We can't see him. We can see
his wife's brunette hair, though, and the red hair of his
nondescript children.

Sometimes a writer wants this detached, omniscient
tone in a story. But most readers read to live vicariously, so
they want to feel the story unfolding. So in the second paragraph, you shift into showing.

One afternoon, John strode through the doorway of
his cozy house and shrugged out of his worn overcoat. The air was sweet with the scent of baking
apples, and Margie's lovely soprano echoed from the
kitchen. Without being told, he knew she was
wearing her red-and-white checked apron, the one
he gave her last Christmas. She always wore it when
she wanted to ask him to do something he wouldn't
want to do.

What did she want this time?

In this paragraph, you have begun to show us John
Smith—we see him shrugging out of his overcoat (instead of
"taking it off"), we smell the baking apples, we hear his
wife's high voice. Then we get a window directly into John's
head—we know he is thinking about his wife and
wondering what she's up to. We can also infer that he's a bit
dictatorial—either that, or this story is set around 1950,

when women wore aprons and pearls to work in the kitchen and men "brought home the bacon."

If, in the next paragraph, you launched into Margie's head, we'd know the story was being told in **omniscient point of view**, where the narrator can see and know all. But if you stay in John's head, we assume you're going to tell this story in **third person**, moving the camera in and out of character's heads as necessary. When writing in third person, be sure to have only one point of view character in each scene.

Showing and point of view are partners. But you can *show* no matter which point of view you've chosen for your story.

If you intend to depict John and Margie having an argument in the next few paragraphs, *show* us details that are pertinent to the scene. Not *every* detail—we don't need to know what kind of pictures are on the wall or what brand of china Margie has in the cupboards. But let us see the twin frown lines between Margie's brows and her hand as it tightens around the handle of the heavy frying pan. Let us hear the crackle of tension in her voice when she says they've been invited to a party at the (red-haired) mayor's house. Show *significant* details to your reader, not every detail in the room.

Is Margie wearing the red-and-white checked apron John gave her last Christmas? If so, you've deepened both of their characters and confirmed John's knowledge of his wife. But if she's wearing a different apron, you've proven John wrong and shown him as an unreliable narrator, at least in this situation.

What is Margie singing? Is she singing "It's Too Late, Baby," "I will Always Love You," or "Jesus Loves Me?"

See how details matter? Is John unnecessarily suspicious, or is Margie hiding something? Does your reader suspect Margie of unfaithfulness, or does your reader think John is too controlling? You, the writer, will shape the reader's thoughts and feelings with the details you provide, so be sure to provide pertinent observations.

This is why we *show* when we want to involve the reader's emotions. By supplying significant details, we evoke certain emotions from our reader and guide their reading experience.

It's that simple. And yes, it means that the majority of your scenes should focus on *showing* your characters and their thoughts as they love, fight, work, argue, debate, ponder, and pray. You will show by letting us see the story through the point of view character's perspective and direct thoughts, through dialogue and observation, and by allowing the reader to make judgments about the objects and situations you've described.

So show us your story world with details and discretion.

HOW TO SHOW

How do you show?

You *show* by using words that evoke the senses while you cut words with which you *tell* the reader.

> Margie turned toward the sink and massaged her left temple, where a headache was beginning to form. Why couldn't John be reasonable? **She heard** her children laughing in the bedroom **and wondered** if he would mention their hair color at dinner. Even though she routinely pointed out that the boys had red-haired cousins, John studied every red-haired male in town with a narrowed gaze.

All right—most of this is showing, but *she heard* is the author telling us that she heard. That sentence would be stronger if we cut *she heard* and wrote *Her children's laughter flowed from the bedroom . . .*

Since we're in Margie's head, we know she's the one hearing. We don't have to remind the reader.

We also know Margie's the one wondering, so we don't need to write *she wondered*. That is clunkier than simply writing her thoughts. We're inside her head, so you don't have to add *she thought, she wondered,* or any other thought attributions. Just write the words in her head. So we could rephrase by writing *Would he mention their hair color at dinner?*

You can avoid such small author intrusions by doing a search for *heard, saw, felt, touched, wondered,* etc., and replacing those words with the same word in all capital letters. As you work through your next draft of the manuscript, look for those phrases and see if you can improve them.

I'm not saying you have to change *every* phrase with those terms, but many times we can make a phrase more descriptive if we take a moment to improve it by showing. In each case, we turn a telling statement into an *action*.

She saw black birds pinwheeling against the sky becomes *Overhead, black birds pinwheeled against the bright sky.*

He heard a gunshot becomes *A shotgun blasted the silence.*

She felt the softness of velvet becomes *Her fingers caressed the velvety softness.*

She tasted the bitterness of gall becomes *Bitterness scalded her tongue.*

Now let's consider what's *right* about the previous paragraph. We see Margie standing at the kitchen sink massaging her temple. Anyone who has ever stood by a kitchen sink will know exactly what that looks like. You don't have to mention the sponge by the faucet or the dishtowel by the dish rack.

And even though we're in Margie's point of view, through her eyes we can see John's gaze narrow whenever he meets a red-haired man, and we are savvy enough to know what he's thinking. Nowhere did you need to write that John suspects his wife of infidelity—all you wrote in the beginning was that he had two red-headed children *whose origin he occasionally questioned.*

For the average adult reader, that's all you need.

DIALOGUE CAN SHOW AND TELL

Dialogue can reveal a lot about a character. A person's words and manner of speaking reveal who he is and where he came from. Even as a British duchess will not use the vocabulary or the accent of a Harlem taxi driver, you can use dialogue and word choice to emphasize the difference between two characters without a word of explanation.

Many writers, including me, have a tendency to create characters that sound alike—probably because our characters are stand-ins for us, so they employ our voices and vocabularies. That's why it's helpful to sketch out character cards for each of your primary story people, noting their educational level and their interests.

Let's say that Anna is a graduate student in English. She's likely to have a strong vocabulary and quote poetry when the mood strikes her.

Her best friend, Jessica, went to work for her father's plumbing company after high school, so she's used to joking around with the plumbers and knows all about couplings and fittings.

Their mutual friend, Michael, works as a runner in a law

office while he attends night school. He's not even close to finishing his degree, but he can talk about lawsuits, filings, briefs, and retainers.

The three friends meet at a park and discuss what they'd like to do that night.

Anna smiles. "I hear *Twelfth Night* is playing at the mall. I'm supposed to read that over the weekend, so I could save some time by watching the movie."

Michael frowns. "Is that the one about the lawyer who has twelve days to get his client out—"

"It's Shakespeare," Anna interrupts. "One of his comedies."

Jessica shakes her head. "No way, Jose. Shakespeare's about as funny as a toilet clog."

"Okay, he's not ha-ha funny, but at least it's not a tragedy. Come on."

"You girls aren't going to out-negotiate me on this one," Michael says. "Either we go see *Righteous Thunder*, or we can go to the diner and have coffee. You aren't going to believe the story I heard in the elevator."

"I don't think you're supposed to discuss what you overhear at work," Anna says. "So let's go to the mall and hang out."

Keep your characters' history, education, occupation, and background in mind as you write dialogue. The better you know your story people, the more convincing your dialogue will be. Your dialogue can do a lot to *show* who your characters are.

One more thing about dialogue. Using anything other than "said" or "asked" in a speaker attribution is almost as bad as adding an adverb or an emotion. Both are examples of the writer calling attention to himself.

"Aw, get outta here," she said, cheekily.
   "Why should I?" he retorted.

Arrrrgh to both of the above!

Having your characters *explain, retort, giggle, laugh, explode, snark, chortle*, or any other word in place of *said* is amateur writing. First, it's physically impossible to speak while you're exploding, giggling, or laughing. Second, it's over the top writing. It's what you wrote in high school to demonstrate that you were creative. Don't do it any more.

Use *said* when absolutely necessary, and don't use anything unless you have to. If a conversation is between two people, you only need an occasional speaker attribution to remind the reader of who is speaking—the indented lines indicate when the speakers change.

With three characters or more, as in the conversation between Anna, Jessica, and Michael, you need to indicate who's speaking, but you can do it with gestures to break up the monotony of "he said" and "she said."

Sometimes I like to look down the left side of a page of dialogue. If I have a "Jackie frowned" at the start of a line followed by a "Michael sighed" in the next paragraph and a "Jackie laughed" in the next, I'll break up that pattern. Be on the lookout for too many similarities in a row.

TURN IMPERSONAL FACTS INTO EMOTIONAL FACTS

In the story we've created so far, we have gathered the following impersonal facts about John and Margie Smith:

They are married.

They live in an ordinary but "cozy" house.

Margie has brown hair.

They have two children with red hair.

Margie sings soprano.

Margie sometimes bakes apples.

John bought Margie a red-and-white checked apron for Christmas.

At least once, Margie has asked John to do something he didn't want to do while wearing that red-and-white-checked apron.

John occasionally wonders about the source of his children's red hair.

Margie suffers from headaches.

John might be jealous.

Not much of a story so far, but we've planted some seeds

that could sprout into interesting developments. Let's consider ways to make the above facts personal for our characters:

> John and Margie are married, but Margie is unhappy.
>
> They live in an ordinary home that is far too small—their children sleep in their bedroom closet, but John refuses to look for a larger house.
>
> Margie's children get their red hair from their grandmother. Margie's mom had flaming red hair, but John never met her.
>
> Margie dreams of singing on stage, but believes John would never support her dream.
>
> Margie bakes apples, but she has been saving the seeds. She knows they contain amygdalin, a substance that releases cyanide when it comes into contact with human digestive enzymes. One day, she thinks, she might need to poison her husband . . .
>
> She hates the apron he bought her for Christmas because every time she wears it he congratulates her for marrying such a generous man.
>
> Every time John jokes about his children's red hair, Margie becomes more determined to keep the secret of her mother's hair color.
>
> John's jealousy and pettiness is literally making Margie ill.

If you write out a series of personal facts about your characters before you begin to write, you can reveal these facts to the reader slowly, one facet at a time. Keep things impersonal at first, and reveal more and more as the story unfolds.

When you consider how much to *show* in a room, a scene, or about a character's clothing, determine which of those details has a personal connection to the character. Perhaps that connection won't be revealed until chapter ten, but the reader will remember it when you mention it again. So mention the objects that either are or will become significant over the course of your story. Those little details will carry a great deal of meaning as your story progresses.

Body language

I'm sure you're familiar with "beats"—the little phrases writers drop into dialogue and character's conversation to keep things from becoming static. Like this scene in John's point of view:

"Welcome home, dear," Margie said, **wiping her hands on her apron. She flashed her husband a quick smile.** "Good day?"

"It was okay." John **set his briefcase by the door and entered the kitchen, then gave his wife a peck on the cheek.** "How about you?"

Margie **bent to open the oven door and peered inside.** "Hmm. It was okay. Little John fell and skinned his knee, and Michael found a dead bird in the back yard. He was upset about that until we had a bird funeral."

"A bird funeral?" John **pressed his lips together,** glad he hadn't been called on to officiate at the sacrilegious occasion. He **sank into a chair at the table.** "What did you do with the corpse?"

She **lifted her brows.** "Why, we buried it, of course." She **closed the oven,** r**an her hand over her**

hair, and flipped it over her shoulder. "Took only a minute."

John folded his hands. "You shouldn't have let the boys near it. Dead animals are filthy."

I have **bolded** the beats in this section. One of them is completely wrong for this scene. Can you spot it and determine why it doesn't fit?

All of the body movements above are natural and normal, particularly for a couple who have been married for a few years. All of them but one—when Margie runs her hand over her hair and flips it. That's a preening gesture, something women do when they are flirting (or if their hair is in their eyes). Margie wouldn't be flirting with John at that moment, especially if he's frowning about something she did to comfort their young son.

When I first started writing, I stuck assorted movements into my dialogue without much thought until I read several books on body language. I quickly learned that most human communication is nonverbal—accomplished not through words, but through facial expression and body movements. As wordsmiths, we don't have the luxury of using fifty words to describe a micro expression, so we use a kind of shorthand to amplify the meaning of movements in dialogue.

I would encourage you to read and study a book on body language, then apply some of those principles to your beats. Here's just a sampling of what you'll learn:

- If a man or woman *folds their arms across their chest*, they are either cold or defensive. They are literally using their arms to build a wall between themselves and someone else.

- If someone crosses only one arm across their chest while the other arm hangs down—they are feeling defensive and insecure. I think of this as the "middle school" pose, because I see it in kids of that age all the time.
- People who are lying will often refuse to meet the eyes of the person they're speaking to. They also have a tendency to touch their necks or noses.
- A boss who calls you into his office, has you sit across from his desk, and then comes around to sit ON the desk is physically reminding you that you are beneath him.
- If a woman touches or flips her hair, she's preening in front of a man she wants to impress.
- If a woman sits on a sofa with one leg tucked under her, the knee of the tucked leg will likely be pointing toward the man she wants to impress.
- If a man enters a room with his thumbs tucked into his belt, he's playing the cocky cowboy and is likely to be a tad aggressive.
- A person who touches your arm while you're talking wants you to hush so he or she can speak.
- A smile that does not make the smiler's eyes crinkle at the corners is more polite than genuine.
- A genuine smile usually shows upper and lower teeth.

Why is it useful for writers to understand basic human body language? Because written body movements can be used to reinforce your prose. Instead of writing, "Margie gave John a genuine smile," which sounds like telling, write

"Margie smiled, the corners of her eyes crinkling." That's showing, giving the reader something to see.

Instead of telling the reader that Margie is feeling defensive by John's criticism of her bird funeral, simply write, "Margie stepped away from the oven and crossed her arms."

Showing that body language gives the reader a picture he will instinctively understand.

So, to edit the above passage, I would write:

She **lifted her brows**. "Why, we buried it, of course."
She **closed the oven and stepped back.** "Took only a minute."

"You shouldn't have let the boys near it. Dead animals are filthy."

Margie crossed her arms. "The boys didn't touch it. And I wore gloves."

No more preening. No need to have John fold his hands as in the original draft—it would have been too much with Margie crossing her arms right after. Margie's movement is stronger.

WHEN TO TELL

Here's the thing—

Showing/telling is not an all-or-nothing proposition. Sometimes, and in some genres, you want to be more generous with description and detail. Sometimes a scene is fast-paced, so you shouldn't slow the action to describe the wallpaper or provide insignificant details. In these cases you combine showing and telling to let the reader know what's happening while simultaneously giving them something to see.

Remember Margie's apple seeds?

Suppose one morning John does something unforgivable, so that afternoon Margie impulsively reaches for the jar where she has been saving apple seeds. Suppose she grinds them into a fine powder and bakes them into a biscuit. Suppose she feeds that biscuit to John during a candlelight dinner while the kids are away at her sister's house. At this point, as John pushes away from the table and grumbles about the dinner, we don't want to slow the pace of the story. We know that within hours, those apple seeds will produce cyanide, John will begin to feel sick, and the poison will begin its work.

How is Margie going to get away with this—or will she?

Suppose John goes into the bedroom and falls asleep, complaining of a stomachache. Margie decides to flee, so she begins to pack a suitcase. We don't want to take the time to describe every item that goes into the suitcase, so we shift into telling. We could give the reader 100 percent telling:

Margie quickly packed a suitcase, ran to the car, and left.

But that does nothing to build a sense of panic, does it? And there's not much for the reader to see.

So let's try something like this:

Margie waited until John's breathing settled into snoring, then she padded to her closet and pulled her suitcase from beneath a row of shoes. Sneakers and heels tumbled as she jerked the luggage out, then opened it on the bedroom floor. She pulled her drawers open, one at a time, grabbing underwear and bras, jeans and tees and the pajamas John hated. Everything went into the suitcase.

In the bathroom she grabbed toothbrush and paste, mascara and lipstick, brush and hair clips and a pony tail elastic. Into the suitcase they went, then she stood in the center of the room, her fingertips tapping her lower lip, eyes searching for anything she might have missed.

When John mumbled in his sleep she froze, rooted to the spot, but when he fell silent she grabbed the suitcase and carried it to the living room, where the click of the latches wouldn't wake him. She slid her feet into the loafers by the door, grabbed her purse, and left the house, heading for her car. Her bag went into the backseat, then she slid into the front, her heart thudding against her breastbone as she slid the key into the ignition.

What was she doing? She had meant to be methodical, perfect in her planning, but John's declaration at breakfast had pressed her into action, sending her into this non-alibied tailspin . . .

She turned the key. She would think things through later, once she was safely away from him.

No great descriptions or details here, just movement, items, and a woman's scattered thoughts as she grabs the necessities she'll need for a night or two away. The writer tells us exactly what Margie does, what she packs, and what she thinks as she drives off.

But even though there's telling, the reader can still see the action. In today's fiction, this is crucial because we write for people who have grown up on television and movies. We are accustomed to seeing movement onscreen and we expect to see it in books as well. So yes, tell me when you need to, but give me things to see while you're telling me.

Unless—

Earlier I mentioned that you may not want to slow the pace of your story (certainly not in a flight scene like this one), and at other times you may not want your readers present for a bit of story action. Why wouldn't you want your readers to see everything?

I remember going to the theater to see *Braveheart*, the story of William Wallace. I knew the story of Wallace, and at the end, as Wallace was being executed, I knew all about the method they used to kill him. Wallace was drawn and quartered, and as that horrific procedure unfolded onscreen, I found myself grimacing—were they actually going to show him being disemboweled?

Thank goodness, they didn't. Though I knew exactly what would have been happening to Wallace, the director kept the camera on Wallace's (Mel Gibson's) face. Though his expression clearly showed agony, fear, and pain, they did not disembowel the character onscreen. I, for one, was grateful.

And as a writer, I know my audience. Though I suspect I am less squeamish than most of my readers, I know there are situations and subjects they will not want to read about. Blood and gore, for one thing. A graphic assault on a woman, for another. Vile language. Anything approaching erotica.

So sometimes I have another character report on something that happened offscreen. When I'm writing about history, I don't deny atrocities that happened, but I don't make my readers sit through the gore, either.

At times like this, telling is not only appropriate, it is a blessing. It is much better to have one character tell another about something that happened than to present it onstage. If you force a reader to endure a scene they find repugnant, they're going to shudder, close the book, and leave a terrible review. Those readers got involved with your characters, they invested the precious minutes of their lives in your story, but you so thoroughly turned them off that they feel cheated.

Trust me—some situations are better told than shown.

For example: In *Rescued Heart*, my novel about Sarah, a marauding army attacked Sodom, where Sarah's brother was living. The attack was fierce and destructive, but I had an escaped servant report the event to Abraham and Sarah:

The former slave, whose face had been hidden by his unkempt hair, raised his head. "Master!" He tried to stand, but stumbled and fell back to the ground.

"Stay where you are," Abram ordered, moving to Oni's

side. He studied the man more closely—someone had tied a bandage around his thigh, and his shaved head was stained with dried blood. The sight tightened Abram's stomach.

"You." Abram gestured to a curious servant. "Bring water, wine, and bread. At once."

As the servant hurried away, Abram sank to the ground beside his friend. "Tell us what happened," he said, urgency sharpening his voice. "Why are you not with Lot?"

Oni lifted his gaze, his eyes haunted by horrors Abram could only imagine. "Your nephew is gone." His voice broke. "All of them—young and old, men and women, even the children have been taken. The city of Sodom has been destroyed. None but the dead and dying remain."

Abram's uneasiness swelled into alarm. "Did my nephew survive?"

"I did not see him, but the dead are scattered throughout the valley of Siddim."

Abram struggled to be patient as Oni guzzled water from a cup.

"Lot," Abram insisted, "has women and children. Does his family live?"

Oni ran his tongue over his chapped lips, wincing at the movement. "I found a dying man among the ruins—he said all who survived the attack were carried away."

"Who took them?"

"Chedorlaomer." Oni shuddered at the name. "He came with a vast army."

Despite the chilly morning air, a drop of sweat carved a path from Abram's armpit to his rib.

I knew it would be more feasible to have the escaped slave, Oni, tell the story of carnage than to actually show it. I knew my readers would not appreciate a blow-by-blow depiction of ancient men lopping off each others' heads.

For the record, however, I did write a scene in that book where Sarah was in a foreign king's harem. Scripture says the Lord closed the wombs of the king's women, so I wrote a scene in which three of the king's concubines were in labor, but the babies would not be born. One of the women died, so the midwife cut the womb in an effort to save the child.

My editor urged me to rewrite that graphic scene, so I did, eliminating the pools of blood and two of the laboring women. I was still able to be true to what happened without turning the stomach of some readers . . . and this is why I appreciate my editors.

WHEN TO NARRATE

Each major character in your novel should have a childhood, of course, and certain events in the backstory of your protagonist will have played a role in the formation of his character. If you want to use one of these events later in your story, perhaps at a climatic moment, reserve that event to show later in a flashback.

But telling *is* appropriate for summarizing a character's backstory.

If you have read any of my other writing lessons, you probably remember that I believe backstory belongs in the back of the story. The first part of your novel is all about hooking your reader with forward momentum, not taking trips down memory lane.

But once you have passed the inciting incident and your character is involved in the story world, you can give the reader more information about your protagonist's background. So let's say that we are well into the story of John and Margie, and the inciting incident occurred when John decided to become an apprentice mortician at the local funeral home. Margie didn't support the idea, but John lost his other job, so she had no choice but to accept his new career.

As John struggles with learning the mortuary business, we might have a scene that begins like this:

Never in a million years had John ever considered working with the dead—how could one make a living from death? But his boss, Maurice Stone, seemed quite content in his role, and frequently quipped that morticians were always assured of job security. "Never forget," he had told John on his first day, "every person you meet in this town may one day be a client."

John managed a weak smile and went back to dusting the caskets, but as he polished the dark veneer of the Heavenly Rest model, his thoughts drifted to a summer day when he was about five. He'd been about to stroke a stuffed cat on the counter of the general store, but his mother shrieked, slapped his hand, and scolded him at the top of her lungs. "That's a dead thing," she cried, her eyes welling with horror. "We never touch dead things!"

John retreated, his arms crossed tight against his chest, and after that he took pains to avoid touching any animal that wasn't moving. He screamed when his father dropped a dead roach into his lap when he was ten, and two years later he fainted straightaway when one of the seventh-grade science students tossed a dead rat onto his desk.

The only bright spot in his middle school years was his mother's willingness to write him a note that excused him from the dissection of any "frog, rat, or other dead creature" that might be required in biology class.

If his mother saw him now, she'd wake every inhabitant of Heavenly Acres Cemetery with her screaming.

Those brief mentions of events in John's past can be narrated—a form of telling that serves to provide important information about the character's backstory. The events with the kitty, the roach, and the rat don't deserve complete scenes of their own, so they can easily be combined in a narration that begins in present time, takes us back to John's childhood (and provides a reason for his reaction to the bird funeral), and brings us back to the story present. But even though the above is narration, notice that it is still visual. The reader can see and hear enough to understand what is happening.

Sometimes narration serves to condense a long period of time into one scene. The following scene from *Rescued Heart* covers the months of Hagar's pregnancy—from the point when Sarah realizes her handmaid is expecting to near the time of Ishmael's birth. It's narration intended to cover several months, but it's still visual and sensory.

How tedious were the days that followed! I had intended to allow Hagar to go about her usual work while I focused on anything but the child in her womb, yet I could think of nothing else. I watched her as a hawk watches a sand rat in the field, with a sharp gaze and eager talons. I snapped at her, jealous because she had conceived while I had not.

Did Abram not tell me that God became jealous when someone took what was rightfully His? In the same way, Hagar had taken what was rightfully mine, and she carried the child meant for me. An inner voice reminded me that I had freely given her the right to take my husband, but she could have attempted to dissuade me. Abram could have protested, but neither of them did.

Resentment nibbled at my confidence and devoured my contentment. I should have been pleased that my plan was successful. I should have been happy that my years of waiting were nearly at an end, but pleasure and happiness remained far from me.

During the ensuing weeks, I gave Hagar more chores than usual, envious because she had earned Abram's affection and gratitude for doing what I had been unable to do. I ignored her when she entered my tent, and I glared if a smile crossed her face. After her fifth month, when the child quickened within her, I often saw her hand on her belly, her eyes alight with wonder at the life within.

In those moments, I wanted to scream.

. . .

One afternoon, I sat on a cushion in my tent, absently tracing the embroidery on my robe. The rhythmic swish-swish of Hagar's broom against the rug was a hypnotic backdrop to my tumultuous thoughts. Each stroke seemed to whisper an accusation: *bar-ren, un-worthy, fail-ure.*

The soothing rhythms suddenly faltered. I looked up, my eyes narrowing as I watched Hagar lean heavily on the broom, her free hand rising to support the unmistakable curve that both fascinated and repulsed me. A groan escaped her lips.

The sight of her standing in my tent, carrying the child that should have been mine, sent a surge of bile into my throat. My fingers clenched, my nails digging into my palms as I struggled to maintain my composure.

"Keep working," I snapped, my voice sounding brittle to my own ears. "The rug is not fully swept."

I expected meek compliance. I should have received it. But as Hagar's eyes met mine, I saw a spark of defiance that had never been there before.

"I am carrying the master's son," she declared, her voice bold and clear. "So do not rebuke me for taking a moment to rest. If you could bear a child, you would understand."

Her words struck me like a slap. The air seemed to leave my lungs, leaving me gasping. A roaring filled my ears, drowning out everything but the echo of those cruel, truthful words: *If you could bear a child*
...

A thousand retorts swarmed to my lips, but they died unspoken, choked by the undeniable truth of her statement.

Another way to impart backstory is to have one character give a summary of his life to another character.

Suppose I'm writing a romance about a young woman who has inherited a farm from her grandfather. The story opens with action, of course, when she looks out on the wheat field and sees a plume of smoke. She jumps into her truck, drives over, and begins to beat a burning patch with a damp blanket. The fire is getting out of hand, but suddenly there is a stranger beside her, helping her extinguish the flames...

All of this would be shown in an active scene, of course.

Many new writers would begin chapter two with the dreaded "backstory dump," where the reader is told that the young woman's grandfather came over from Europe in 1975, bought the land, and worked it for years. And how he married and lost four children before having her father, who married her mother, etc., etc., but before Grandpa died he made our young heroine promise to never sell the farm because it had to remain in the family.

But we're going to cut that entire second chapter. Backstory does not belong in the front of the book.

So *our* second chapter should begin with our lovely heroine thanking the handsome stranger for helping her, and they gather up the wet blankets and she offers him a glass of lemonade back at the house, and he is pleased to accept. So the next scene shows them sitting in the kitchen, tired and soaked in soot and sweat, but smiling, and she says she'll never be able to repay him, and he says, "Well, maybe you can. If you know of someone looking for a handyman or helper, I'm looking for work."

Then our young heroine says, "Well . . . you know, since I inherited this place, I've been struggling to manage on my own. So sure, you can sleep in the room above the barn, and I can pay you by the week."

That's all the backstory we really need right now, just a mention of how she got the farm and why she's working it alone.

So the book continues and the hero and heroine fall in love, and about three-quarters of the way through they get through a really big challenge (taxes, or a storm, or maybe the expensive pregnant mare dies while foaling), and they realize they really love each other, and the hero proposes . . . and the heroine says no.

And the reader is stunned, and you have created tension *because you cut chapter two.* The reader doesn't know about the promise she made to her dying grandfather.

So then you insert the significant scene, filled with emotional detail, of how she rushed home from college to be at her dying grandpa's side, and how his gnarled hand took hers, and how he hoarsely asked that she make him a promise.

"Anything, Grandpa," she whispered.

And he made her promise not to sell the farm. Which means she can't marry the handsome hero, because he's already told her he's set on moving to Montana and buying a ranch ...

Do you see how much more significant that backstory is when it is 1) shown in detail and 2) reserved for a key emotional moment and not offered to the reader up front?

I don't know how that story ends, but if it's a genre romance, they'll work it out and get together. Maybe a long lost cousin will arrive to take over the family farm, or maybe the hero will decide that a farm is as fulfilling as a ranch. But genre romance requires a happy ending, so they'll get one.

TELLING GONE WRONG

Sometimes we fall prey to the impulse to explain things in speaker attributions.

"What's wrong?" Margie asked, *bewildered*.

Margie's bewilderment needs to be obvious in her dialogue and actions, not in your speaker attributions. So if Margie is watching John pace back and forth in the living room, instead of *telling* us she's bewildered, write:

"Forty-two," Margie announced.
John stopped pacing. "Forty-two what?"
"You've walked past me forty-two times in the last fifteen minutes. What is wrong with you?"

One of the most cringe-worthy things new writers do to *tell* is insert the dreaded "as you know, Bob" into dialogue. I once read a book and bloodied the margin with scrawling when I read:

"Yes, Bob, I know we're living on an island where the ferry comes only at ten a.m. and four p.m., but . . ."

I knew right then that something bad was going to happen, but the characters wouldn't be able to get off the island because the ferry wasn't there. The writer had told me so in one of the clumsiest ways imaginable.

Don't have your characters tell each other things they already know. Writers do it to impart information to readers, but the most effective way is to have a newcomer enter the scene, someone who doesn't know the basics of life in your story world. A friendly character can gradually release the information the newcomer—and your reader—needs to know. Just make sure there's a valid reason for the newcomer to be in the story.

SHOW EMOTIONAL CHANGES

Most novels achieve a balance between plot and character. Readers expect a plot to drive the actions of the characters, and character changes to influence plot. Yet some novels (*Driving Miss Daisy, Steel Magnolias, Postcards from the Edge*) are more about character than plot; other novels are completely about plot with little character change. James Bond, for instance, isn't about personal maturation; he's about saving the world.

But in writing your novel, you can't assume that the reader realizes how your character is changing over the course of the novel. Your character shouldn't change all at once—things happen, and though he may cling to his stubborn ways at first, eventually he must change.

A good way to show a character's realization of his need to change is to use the "A month before . . . but now" construction. You can write two paragraphs or two pages, but the idea is that the character takes a look at his life and realizes that he needs to change.

Let's say that Margie's attempt to poison John didn't work—he got a little sick, threw up his dinner, and then realized that Margie had left him. That was the wake-up call he needed to change.

So we write:

Two weeks ago, he had taken Margie for granted—belittling her efforts with the boys, suspecting her of being unfaithful, and not listening to her desires. Why, he'd been more respectful toward his boss than his wife!

But now, facing his empty house, seeing that cheap red-and-white checked apron hanging on a nail by the pantry door, he realized what a lousy husband he'd been. No wonder Margie had gone. He had given her no reason to stay.

In Dickens' *A Christmas Carol* we meet the ultimate curmudgeon, Ebenezer Scrooge. At the beginning, Scrooge is a stingy, hard-hearted man who cares nothing for Christmas or his fellow man. The ghost of his dead partner, Jacob Marley, appears to warn Scrooge that he will be visited by three spirits during the night, and though Scrooge is frightened, he goes to bed grumbling.

The first spirit, the Ghost of Christmas Past, shows Scrooge as a young boy who dearly loved his sister. Watching as his past plays out before him, Scrooge is warmed by his memories and weeps when the woman he loves, Belle, breaks up with him because he loves money more than her. We see his tears, but he does not change in a major way.

The second spirit, the Ghost of Christmas Present, shows Scrooge what is happening across town—his clerk, Bob Cratchit, is celebrating with his family, trying to feed his family festive meal on the small salary Scrooge pays him.

Bob's youngest son, known as Tiny Tim, shivers in the corner, sick, but determined to be happy. In another house Scrooge also sees his nephew, the now-grown son of his dearly departed sister, celebrating with his bride. The occasion is so festive and happy that Scrooge begs the spirit to linger in that place for a while. Just before the Spirit leaves, he shows Scrooge two starving children, Ignorance and Want.

The third spirit appears, a mute Ghost of Christmas Yet to Come. Scrooge sees businessmen discussing the recent death of a wealthy man whose riches did no one any good. He sees a cleaning woman selling bed curtains in a marketplace, and suddenly realizes they are *his* bed curtains. Then he is led to a gravestone, and realizes that it must be his own.

Over the course of the story Dickens shows us that Scrooge was once a happy man and that he does have feelings. We have seen his delight in his family and finally we see Scrooge's horror at realizing what will eventually become of him. If he does not change, he will be mourned by no one, loved by no one, and his life will have had no meaning.

In terms of the Plot Skeleton,[1] this is the bleakest moment, when Scrooge has no hope. But the Spirit of Christmas Yet to Come sends Scrooge back to the present, where he internalizes his lesson and decides to renounce his stingy ways and honor the Spirit of Christmas for the rest of his life. He wakes in his own bed, with the curtains still in place.

---

1. The Plot Skeleton is the first of the Writing Lessons from the Front Series. It provides a quick but thorough overview of the elements of plotting.

But Dickens knew it was not enough for Scrooge to simply *say* he was going to change. A good writer must *show* the reader that the character has changed; that the events of the story have changed him for good and forever.

So at the end of *A Christmas Carol*, we see Scrooge buying the biggest, fattest goose at the market for the Cratchit family. We see him giving the errand boy who delivers the goose a generous tip. We see him go to his nephew's house, where he begs forgiveness for his past indifference and is invited to join them for Christmas dinner.

Then the narrator tells us that Scrooge becomes "like a father" to Tiny Tim, and helps him get well. And the ending is so strong, so powerful that I'm crying as I'm typing this— excuse me while I blow my nose—and the reader takes the lesson that Scrooge learned to his or her own heart.

Like Dickens, we must show our protagonist's change in increments. And then, once our main character has learned his or her lesson and made a decision to live differently, we must show them living and reacting in in a way that would have been impossible for them at the beginning of the story. If you're following the plot skeleton, this is the *resolution*, and it doesn't have to be long—a scene or two, or an epilogue, can show that the life change was permanent.

IN SUMMARY

If you're concerned that you're telling rather than showing, ask yourself these questions:

1. If a scene will lead to an emotional response, are you allowing the reader to see what's going on? Is there something to see, hear, taste, touch, or smell? I wouldn't use all five senses in a shorter scene—those details might become distracting or heavy-handed—but three out of five isn't too much.

2. Are you showing in great detail a scene that has little relevance to the protagonist's character or situation? Would it be better to tell and/or summarize this information?

3. Have you kept the protagonist's backstory out of the beginning of the story? Have you waited at least until after the inciting incident to provide details of his or her past? Have you reserved the most life-changing and emotional event of his past to use later (if necessary) and show in great detail?

4. Are you, the writer, breaking into the the story by telling us about what the character is sensing or feeling?

Can you silence yourself by using an action to help the reader understand what the character is feeling?

5. Are you are naming emotions (He felt sad . . . or sadness overwhelmed him) instead of conveying the emotion by the character's actions?

Remember, most people react to situations with a mixture of emotions. A man whose daughter has been killed in a car accident may experience many feelings when he hears the news: grief, guilt, anger, fear, even hysterical laughter. Even love can be a mixture of joy, warmth, anxiety, jealousy, and fear. One cannot love without risk . . .

6. Are you inserting emotional states into your speaker attributions? ("What's wrong?"she asked, confused.) Make sure you remove those.

7. Does your characters' speech reflect their status, educational level, and background? If one character is very different from the others, make sure his dialogue is different, too. While you're examining dialogue, be sure to keep your speaker attributions simple. Let the dialogue do the work.

8. Remember—sometimes you tell, sometimes you show, sometimes you narrate, and sometimes you do a mixture of telling and showing, depending upon the pace of your scene. But whatever you do, give your reader something to see. The modern reader expects to *see* a story unfold.

EXERCISES

1. On a separate sheet of paper, jot down the major events of your life from ages ten through fifteen. Now imagine yourself as the protagonist of a novel. Which of those events would you summarize and tell, which would you narrate, and which would you show? Hint: the *emotional* element is the key.

2. Think of the last movie you watched. *Tell* us the story in one paragraph.

3. Now think of the most emotional scene in that particular movie. Write out that scene as if you were writing it in a novel, showing us everything that happened and revealing what the characters were feeling.

4. Let's evolve a sentence from pure telling to vibrant showing.

- John was frightened.
- John's hand shook as he set the kettle on to boil.
- As he set the kettle on to boil, John's hand shook and his thoughts raced.

- After setting the kettle on the gas stove, John's hand trembled as he powered on the flame. His thoughts raced. What weapons did he have at hand? The menacing stranger stood only three feet away.
- Your turn!

5. Let's say you are writing a nonfiction book on how prion diseases (like mad cow) affect the brain. You have found this paragraph describing CJD:

> Creutzfeldt–Jakob disease, also known as subacute spongiform encephalopathy or neurocognitive disorder due to prion disease, is a fatal neurodegenerative disease. Early symptoms include memory problems, behavioral changes, poor coordination, and visual disturbances. Later symptoms include dementia, involuntary movements, blindness, weakness, and coma. About 70% of people die within a year of diagnosis.[1]

Write a paragraph describing the scientific process in which prions invade the brain cells and begin to take over. (If you can't guess at the process, make it up. The point here is to choose the best method of relaying the information. Because you're writing facts, you should *tell*.)

Now that you've *told* us about CJD, because this nonfiction book is not for scientists, you need to reach regular people. So how would you write about living with a family member

---

1. {$NOTE_LABEL}. https://en.wikipedia.org/wiki/Creutzfeldt–Jakob_disease, Wikipedia, accessed January 7, 2025.

who has been diagnosed with CJD? In this case, you would *show*, so use the information above to illustrate what that would be like.